Football Files

GOALKEEPER

Michael Hurley

www.raintreepublishers.co.uk
Visit our website to find out more information about Raintree books.

To order:

☎ Phone 0845 6044371

▤ Fax +44 (0) 1865 312263

⌨ Email myorders@raintreepublishers.co.uk

Customers from outside the UK please telephone +44 1865 312262

Raintree is an imprint of Capstone Global Library Limited, a company incorporated in England and Wales having its registered office at 7 Pilgrim Street, London, EC4V 6LB – Registered company number: 6695582

Edited by Louise Galpine, Vaarunika Dharmapala, and John-Paul Wilkins
Designed by Philippa Jenkins
Original illustrations © Capstone Global Library Ltd 2010
Illustrated by KJA-artists.com
Picture research by Hannah Taylor
Originated by Capstone Global Library Ltd
Printed and bound in China by Leo Paper Products Ltd

ISBN 978 1 406216 39 4 (hardback)
14 13 12 11 10
10 9 8 7 6 5 4 3 2 1

British Library Cataloguing in Publication Data
Hurley, Michael
Goalkeeper. -- (Football files)
796.3'3426-dc22
A full catalogue record for this book is available from the British Library.

Acknowledgements
We would like to thank the following for permission to reproduce photographs: Action Images pp. **14** (Stuart Franklin), **28** (The FA/David Cerny); Corbis pp. **9** (epa/Jesus Diges), **11** (Hulton-Deutsch Collection), **17** (Reuters/Alessandro Garofalo), **16** (epa/Roland Weihrauch), **25** (Reuters/Dylan Martinez), **24** (Christian Liewig); Getty Images pp. **5** (Clive Brunskill), **18** (Bob Thomas), **27** (AFP/Jose Luis Roca); © KPT Power Photos background image; Press Association pp. **8** (Empics/Mike Egerton), **6** (Empics), **10** (AP Photo/Bippa), **12** (Empics/Alejandro Fernandez), **20** (Empics/Ross Kinnaird), **21** (Empics/Neal Simpson), **23** (Empics/Mike Egerton); Shutterstock **background image** (© Nikola I).

Cover photograph of Iker Casillas diving during the 2008 UEFA quarter-final match between Spain and Italy, Ernst Happel stadium, Vienna, Austria, reproduced with permission of Corbis/Christian Liewig.

We would like to thank Dr Sarah Schenker for her invaluable help in the preparation of this book.

Every effort has been made to contact copyright holders of material reproduced in this book. Any omissions will be rectified in subsequent printings if notice is given to the publisher.

CONTENTS

Some words are shown in bold, **like this**. You can find out what they mean by looking in the glossary on page 30.

Football is the most popular sport in the world. Nearly every country has a **professional** football **league**. Even countries that don't have professional leagues and professional players still have lots of people playing football just for fun and exercise. A football can be created out of anything – even a rolled up sock! This means that football can be played anywhere and by anyone.

Organized football matches have two teams with eleven players on each side. Each team is made up of players who have different positions and roles on the pitch. The goalkeeper's main job is to stop the **opposition** team from scoring a goal.

Fair play in football

Fair play (also called sportsmanship) is important in every sport. Fair play means following the rules of the game, and behaving honestly and respectfully towards the people you are playing with.

In a Premiership match between Everton and West Ham United in 2000 there was an amazing moment of sportsmanship. As West Ham attacked Everton, the Everton goalkeeper came rushing out of the **penalty box** to clear the ball. As he made the clearance he fell awkwardly and was obviously injured. The match continued and a West Ham player crossed the ball into the penalty area.

This player was hoping that a teammate would take advantage of the goalkeeper being out of action and score a goal. As the ball came across, however, instead of trying to score, West Ham's Paolo Di Canio caught the ball in his hands – ending play. His gesture was well received by the opposition players and supporters.

The goalkeeper can use any part of his body to **deflect** the ball away from the goal. He can use his hands to catch the ball or punch it. He can use his feet to kick the ball. He can use his head to clear the ball away from the goal if he cannot catch or punch it. The goalkeeper is the only player who can touch the ball with his hands during a match. He can do this only when he is inside the penalty box.

You need certain skills to be a really good goalkeeper. Goalkeepers need to be extremely **agile** and have very good **reactions**. They need to be able to catch and handle the ball confidently. Many of the best goalkeepers are also tall and strong.

Paul Robinson, of Blackburn Rovers, tries to make a diving save in a match against Everton in 2009.

IKER CASILLAS

Iker Casillas is the goalkeeper for Real Madrid and Spain. He joined Real Madrid when he was 8 years old and played his **debut** match for them when he was 18. For the past decade Casillas has been one of their most **consistent** and important players.

"Saint Iker"

The fans call him "San Iker", which means Saint Iker, for his outstanding **contribution** to the club on and off the pitch. He has made so many amazing saves in the last 10 years that the supporters expect him to play well in every match. He does not usually disappoint them.

This is Iker Casillas in one of his early appearances for Real Madrid. He has now played in more than 450 matches for the club.

NARROWING THE ANGLE

One of Iker Casillas' best skills is his ability to close down the **opposition**. He will rush out from his goal and try to put the opposition player off. At the same time, he is making the angle narrow and therefore more difficult for the player to score from.

1. An attacker approaches the goal with the ball. The goalkeeper moves out towards the attacker.

2. The goalkeeper stays upright and spreads his body to block as much of the goal as possible from the attacker's view.

3. The goalkeeper dives for the ball. He gets his hands on it and quickly gathers it to his body.

Iker Casillas uses his feet to save a shot from Bayer Leverkusen's Dimitar Berbatov (right) during the 2002 Champions League final.

Winning trophies

In 2000, in his second **season**, Casillas won the **UEFA** Champions League. This was an amazing achievement for the young goalkeeper. In fact, he was the youngest ever goalkeeper to play in a Champions League final.

In the 2001/02 season he didn't play quite so well, and a more experienced goalkeeper replaced him on the team. When Real Madrid got to the UEFA Champions League final, though, Casillas had to come on as a **substitute** to play the last 20 minutes of the match. Casillas made a series of outstanding saves to ensure that Real Madrid won the trophy. The score was 2–1 to Real Madrid against Bayer Leverkusen. From that moment on he would be the first choice goalkeeper at the Santiago Bernabeau, the home of Real Madrid.

International career

Casillas' international career began in 2000 after he had played an important role in helping Spain win the **FIFA** Under 20 World Cup **tournament**. He has now played more than 100 times for his country and was part of the Spanish team that won the UEFA European Championships in 2008.

Casillas' incredible consistency, **agility**, and calm approach make him one of the best and most successful goalkeepers in the world. He signed a new contract with Real Madrid in 2008, which should keep him at the club until 2017, when he will be 36 years old. He said: "I joined Real Madrid as a child and Madrid is my home."

Iker Casillas (left) and his Real Madrid teammate Sergio Ramos celebrate winning a Spanish First Division League match in 2008.

LEV YASHIN

Lev Yashin is one of the best goalkeepers in football history. He was born in Moscow in Russia, in 1929. During World War II (1939–1945), he went to work in a local factory. He was just 12 years old. He joined the factory football team.

After the war, Yashin joined Dynamo Moscow's youth team. For a few years he was second choice to a very good goalkeeper and had to be patient for his chance to play. Then, in 1949 he was invited to join the **first team** by the coach. Yashin made his **debut** in 1950. He played in goal for Dynamo Moscow for 22 years.

Lev Yashin makes a diving save for the **USSR** (CCCP in Russian) during the 1966 World Cup.

The Black Spider

Yashin was tall and **athletic** and he had long arms and long fingers. This meant that he was able to reach some shots that other goalkeepers wouldn't have been able to. His supporters and **opponents** gave him the nickname "Black Spider". He always wore a black kit and his arms and legs seemed to be able to stop all the shots at his goal.

In his long career Yashin made more than 400 appearances for club and country. He is also reported to have made about 150 penalty saves!

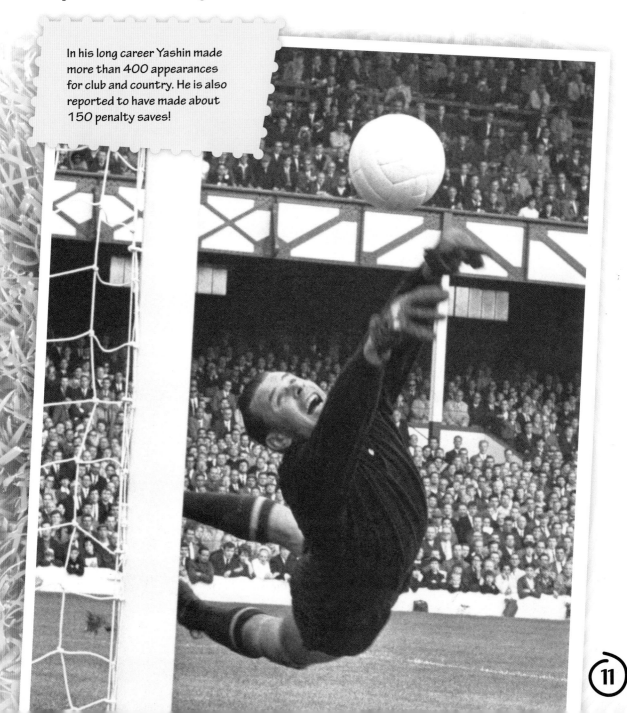

International debut

Yashin made his international debut for the USSR in 1954. He was the USSR goalkeeper at the 1956 Olympic Games in which they won a gold medal. In 1960 he helped the USSR to win the **UEFA** European Championships (then known as the European Nations Cup). His performances over the next few years were so outstanding that he was named the 1963 European Footballer of the Year. He is still the only goalkeeper to have ever won the award.

Health and fitness

Lev Yashin was a smoker. In the 1940s and 1950s this was not unusual. Today, however, footballers rarely smoke. Smoking can damage a footballer's performance on the field, making him short of breath. It can also lead to many diseases such as cancer, heart disease, and lung disease.

The award for the best goalkeeping performance at the FIFA World Cup is named after Lev Yashin. Winners include Germany's Oliver Kahn (pictured) and France's Fabian Barthez.

Training hard

Yashin was always training and practising to make sure he performed at a high standard. He was very determined and hated the **opposition** scoring goals against him. He once said: "What kind of goalkeeper is the one that is not tormented by the goal he has allowed? He must be tormented!"

PENALTIES

One of Yashin's greatest skills was his ability to save **penalties**. When trying to save a penalty it is important to watch the opposition player and try to **anticipate** where he is going to shoot. Your **reactions** need to be very good as well. If you move too soon the opposition player will just shoot the ball into the open space that you have left in the goal.

1. An attacker is lining up his penalty shot.

2. Before the attacker kicks the ball, the goalkeeper tries to anticipate which direction he will shoot in.

3. The attacker kicks the ball to the left. The goalkeeper has dived in the right direction and saves the penalty.

GIANLUIGI BUFFON

Gianluigi Buffon is one of the most famous goalkeepers in the world. He plays for Juventus and Italy. Buffon comes from a successful sporting family. His mother was a discus and shot-put champion in Italy and his father was also a shot-putter. Buffon's two older sisters are volleyball players. Buffon says: "Since the beginning, my family helped me to express myself through sport."

Starting young

From an early age Buffon was interested in football. He joined a local football school when he was six years old. When he played for the school's team he was a **midfielder** and not a goalkeeper. When he was 12, Buffon started to play for another football team and changed his position to goalkeeper. This was the beginning of a very successful career.

Gianluigi Buffon has been named "World Goalkeeper of the Year" four times so far in his career. He has also been awarded the title of "Serie A (Italian League) Goalkeeper of the Year" an amazing eight times.

ANTICIPATION AND POSITIONING

Buffon is very good at **anticipating** what will happen next on the football pitch and when he will need to spring into action. With good anticipation and positioning you can make it difficult for the **opponent** to score. If a **cross** comes in, the goalkeeper must keep his eye on the ball. He must also be aware of the **opposition** players who are waiting for the cross to reach them. Good positioning can help the goalkeeper to intercept the ball before it reaches the opposition player.

1. A player is lining up a cross to a waiting striker (in red), who is being closely watched by a defender. The goalkeeper is in position in front of the goal.

2. The player kicks the ball to the striker who prepares to head it. The goalkeeper positions himself in front of the striker and prepares to catch the ball.

3. The goalkeeper has anticipated the direction of the ball and successfully catches it.

Getting noticed

When Buffon was just 13 years old, his talent as a goalkeeper was noticed by some of the biggest and most successful football teams in Italy. He had an offer to join AC Milan, but instead chose to join Parma, as they were closer to his home. He worked hard to improve his **technique** and **physique**. After a few years he got his chance to play for the **first team**. At 17 he made his **debut** for Parma against AC Milan. He played well and managed to keep a **clean sheet**. He would soon become Parma's first choice goalkeeper.

Gianluigi Buffon celebrates after the final of the 2006 FIFA World Cup between Italy and France. Italy won 5–3 in the penalty shoot-out.

Moving on

In the next 6 years Buffon made more than 160 appearances for Parma. He was part of a successful team that won the **UEFA** Cup, Italian Cup, and Italian Super Cup. After so much success at Parma, Buffon decided it was time to move on. There were a lot of football clubs interested in him. In the summer of 2001 Buffon moved to Juventus for a world record transfer fee for a goalkeeper. Juventus paid Parma £32 million for him. After such an expensive transfer, there was a lot of pressure on Buffon. He did not let it show as he helped Juventus win the **league** in his first season.

Health and fitness

Buffon has suffered a couple of injuries during his career. His **dedication** and training have helped him to recover from injuries. In 2000 he missed the UEFA European Championships because he had a broken finger. This type of injury is not unusual for goalkeepers as they often come into violent contact with the ball. That is why it is very important to wear gloves when you are playing in goal (see page 25).

Gianluigi Buffon, seen here making a save in a warm-up session, stayed loyal to Juventus when they were demoted to the Italian second division in 2006. He helped his team return to Serie A the following season.

DAVID SEAMAN

David Seaman is a **legend** of English football. He started his career at Leeds United, the team he supported as a child. He did not manage to break into the **first team**. Seaman joined Peterborough United, in the lowest division in England. Some players would have settled for this, but Seaman was determined to show what a good goalkeeper he could be.

Working hard

Seaman's **consistent** performances attracted attention from other football clubs and he soon joined a team in a higher division. Birmingham City signed him in 1984 and he helped them win promotion to the top division in English football. After two years with Birmingham, Seaman was bought by Queens Park Rangers, where he showed off his natural ability and bravery. Arsenal signed Seaman in 1990, for a British transfer record (for a goalkeeper) of £1.3 million. With hard work and **dedication** he had made it to one of the most **prestigious** and successful teams in English football.

David Seaman made a name for himself as a good, consistent goalkeeper during his time at Birmingham City.

BALL HANDLING

David Seaman was known for his bravery and his ball-handling ability. Good ball handling is essential for all goalkeepers. You can practise your ball-handling skills by facing the goal and then turning around and trying to catch a ball that is kicked towards you. Try to repeat this 10 times and see how many you can catch.

1. The goalkeeper has his back to the attacker, who is lining up a shot.

2. The attacker kicks the ball and the goalkeeper spins around to catch it.

3. The goalkeeper reacts well to the shot and he is able to catch the ball.

Ups and downs at Arsenal

Arsenal won the **league** in Seaman's first **season**. He **conceded** only 18 goals in 38 matches to help his team achieve this. It was the beginning of a spell of great success for Seaman and his team. Arsenal won the League Cup and FA Cup two seasons later, and won the **UEFA** Cup-Winner's Cup in 1994. At this time, Seaman was regarded as one of the world's top goalkeepers.

Arsenal made it to the final of the Cup-Winner's Cup for the second season in a row. The match finished badly for Seaman. In the last minute he **misjudged** a shot and it went over his head into the goal. Arsenal lost the match and Seaman was criticized for his mistake. He managed to ignore the criticism and continue to perform consistently well for Arsenal for the next eight years. Seaman's last game for Arsenal was the FA Cup final in 2003, which they won.

In the UEFA Cup Winners Cup final in 1995 David Seaman made a mistake that led to Arsenal losing the match. It is very important for goalkeepers to overcome any mistakes they make and try not to repeat them in future matches.

Playing for England

Seaman made his **debut** for England in 1988. By 1994 he was the first choice England goalkeeper. In 1996 England played in the UEFA European Championships. Seaman helped England to have a good **tournament**. He made some crucial **penalty** saves in the group stage and quarter-final. Unfortunately, he could not repeat this in the semi-final against Germany, and England were knocked out on penalties. Seaman's excellent performances meant that he was given the "Player of the Tournament" award. It is very unusual for a goalkeeper to win this award.

David Seaman, in action for Arsenal, makes a save and holds on to the ball.

Safe hands!

David Seaman was given the nickname "Safe Hands" by his Arsenal and England teammates. They gave him this nickname because they knew that he was a great goalkeeper who could always be relied upon.

PETR ČECH

Petr Čech is the Chelsea and Czech Republic goalkeeper. He is considered to be one of the top goalkeepers in the world. He began his career at his local football club and soon moved to one of the top teams in the Czech Republic, Sparta Prague. While he was at Sparta, Čech broke the national goalkeeping record for the number of **clean sheets** in a **season**. He attracted interest from teams across Europe, and transferred to Rennes, in France, in 2002.

SHOT STOPPING

Petr Čech makes lots of diving saves to stop the **opposition** scoring. He makes sure that he is positioned correctly so that he can jump in any direction to make a save. You can practise diving saves with a friend. While you are in goal, your friend can take shots from different angles. If you are in the right position, you should be able to stop the shots by diving to catch the ball.

1. The goalkeeper is standing on his toes, ready to move in any direction.

2. Keeping his eyes on the ball, he pushes off from his right foot to start diving to his left.

3. He stretches out his arms and spreads his fingers to get his hands behind the ball.

4. He gathers the ball into his body to prevent it from spilling out as he lands on the ground.

Petr Čech (far left) celebrates with his teammates and manager after winning the English Premier League in 2005.

Success at Chelsea

Čech continued to improve, and in the summer of 2004 he signed for Chelsea for £7 million. This was a club record transfer fee for a goalkeeper. Čech's first season with Chelsea was remarkable, and he made some amazing saves. Chelsea won the Premier League for the first time. Čech broke the Premier League record for the number of clean sheets in a season and also the record for fewest goals **conceded**. He was awarded the "Golden Gloves" award for the best goalkeeper in the Premier League.

Playing for his country

After helping the Czech Republic win the **UEFA** Under 21 European Championships in 2002, Čech became first choice goalkeeper for the national team. He has played more than 70 times for his country. At the 2004 European Championships Čech produced some outstanding performances. The Czech Republic missed out on the final, losing 1-0 to Greece in extra-time, in the semi-final..

Health and fitness

Petr Čech suffered a horrible injury during a match in 2006. He was caught on the side of the head by an **opponent's** knee. His skull was fractured and he needed an operation. It was very serious and he could have died. He took a long time to recover and he had to train very hard to return to the Chelsea team. To avoid getting hurt in the same way again Čech now wears a protective head guard during matches.

Petr Čech, wearing his head guard, dives through the air to make a save during a match for Chelsea in 2009.

Petr Čech is a tall, agile goalkeeper. He can make outstanding saves. Here, he is in action for Chelsea, at full stetch, tipping the ball over the goal.

Goalkeeper's gloves

For many years goalkeepers did not have any protection for their hands. They could get injuries to their fingers, palms, and wrists. Today, professional goalkeepers wear protective gloves. As well as protecting the goalkeeper from injury, the gloves also help them to hold on to the ball. Modern goalkeeper gloves are made of strong, lightweight materials. The palms of the gloves are made out of latex, which gives the goalkeeper a lot of protection. The latex palms also give very good levels of grip, even in bad weather conditions.

Training

Goalkeepers are usually trained separately from the rest of their team. A lot of teams have an ex-goalkeeper who works as a **coach** with the goalkeepers.

Before training and before matches goalkeepers need to do a lot of stretches to help them to be flexible and **agile**.

Goalkeepers go to the gym to lift weights. This helps them to improve their strength. It is important for them to be able to take a few knocks during a match.

Goalkeepers also do some running work. This helps them with their **stamina** during a match.

Repetition is a big part of a goalkeeper's training. They have to repeat handling exercises and practise saving shots that come from different angles. It is important for them to practise making saves from shots along the ground and also from shots that come in at different heights.

Fenerbahce's Volkam Demirel is trying to take up as much of the goal as he can to make it difficult for his **opponent** to score.

Stance

When playing in goal make sure that you stand with you legs shoulder-width apart, with your knees slightly bent. You should be standing on the balls of your feet (on your toes), so that you are ready to make a save at any moment during a match. You must stay alert and concentrate all through the match.

This goalkeeper stays focused and keeps her eyes on the ball as she prepares to make a save.

Catching

When catching a football try to get your body behind the ball. If you make a mistake with your catching, the ball will hit your body rather than going past you into the goal. Goalkeepers should always try to catch the ball, but sometimes it is not possible. Instead of catching, some goalkeepers punch the ball away from the goal.

Diving saves

Sometimes, when an opponent shoots at the goal, the goalkeeper has to make a diving save. As the goalkeeper, it is important that you **anticipate** the direction of the shot, and are ready to dive in the same direction. Keep your eyes on the ball and dive across the goal towards the ball. Try to catch the ball if you can, or push it away from the goal.

Distribution

The goalkeeper is often the player who distributes (gives) the ball to other members of his team. Good distribution of the football is crucial for a goalkeeper and his team. When a goalkeeper has control of the ball during a match he can either kick it or throw it. He must be accurate with his distribution, so that the ball makes its way to a teammate and not the opposition.

Coming off the line

Goalkeepers need to be able to come off the goal line quickly to make saves. To learn how to do this, you can practise sprinting over short distances with some friends. Divide into two teams, with each team lined up 10 metres away from a cone. Have a relay race around the cones and back. This is also a good **warm-up** before you start to play football.

Handling

Handling is a very important skill for a goalkeeper. They must watch the ball at all times and try to catch it with both hands. They must gather the ball safely in to their bodies. If they drop it, the **opposition** gains another chance to score.

Pass back

When receiving a pass from a teammate the goalkeeper is not allowed to touch the ball with his hands. If he does, it is a **foul** and the opposition get a **free kick**.

GLOSSARY

agile able to move quickly and easily

anticipate perform before another player has a chance to react

athletic physically active and strong. Professional sportspeople are usually athletic.

clean sheet no goals. If a goalkeeper does not let in a goal during a match, he has kept a clean sheet.

coach person who organizes and takes training sessions to help the team to prepare for a match

concede allow. If a goalkeeper concedes a goal, he allows it to pass into the net.

consistent always the same

contribution part played by a person in making something happen. The goalkeeper's contribution to a game is in stopping the other team from scoring.

cross kicking the ball from one side of the pitch to a player in the middle, usually near the goal

debut first time that a player plays for a team

dedication caring a lot about something and working hard for it. A dedicated player works hard for his or her team.

deflect cause something, for example a football, to change direction

FIFA (*Fédération Internationale de Football Association*) international organization responsible for football around the world

first team first choice line-up of players who start the match

foul when a player breaks one of the rules of football. A foul could be a mis-timed tackle or a deliberate trip.

free kick kick of the ball awarded by the referee after a foul

league group of teams that play against each other during the football season. There are national football leagues all over the world.

legend extremely famous person who is well-known for their particular talent or success

midfielder position of a player on the pitch. Midfielders link the attacking and defending players.

misjudge get something wrong

opponent/opposition person or team that you are playing against

penalty the referee gives a penalty if a foul happens in the 18-yard box. The ball is placed on a spot 12 yards from goal and only the goalkeeper is allowed to stop the shot.

penalty box area around the goal, also known as the 18-yard box

physique form or structure of a person's body

prestigious something that is very important or special

professional being paid to do something. Professional footballers earn a salary for playing football.

reaction response to something

season length of time that a league runs for

stamina ability to take part in physical activity for a long time

substitute players who do not start a match but who can replace a player on the pitch. Three substitutes can be used in most matches.

technique way of doing something. Different players control the ball in different ways on the pitch, and there is good and bad technique for certain passes and skills.

tournament organized number of matches that lead to a final. The winner of the final game wins the tournament.

UEFA (Union of European Football Associations) organization responsible for European football

USSR (Union of Soviet Socialist Republics) union of Eastern European countries which broke up in 1991

warm-up gentle exercises that are done before starting a tiring physical activity

FIND OUT MORE

Books to read

Usborne Activities: 50 Soccer Skills, Jonathan Sheikh-Miller (Usborne, 2008)

Essential Sports: Football, Andy Smith (Heinemann Library, 2008)

Skills (Know the Game): Soccer – Goalkeeping (A&C Black, 2007)

Sport Files: Wayne Rooney, John Townsend (Raintree, 2009)

The World Cup series, Michael Hurley (Heinemann Library, 2009)

Websites

http://www.thefa.com/skills

The website of the English Football Association. This site has lots of videos to help you improve your skills and technique.

http://news.bbc.co.uk/sport2/hi/academy/default.stm

The BBC Sport Academy website includes videos and tutorials to help you learn more about playing football.

http://www.fifa.com/aboutfifa/developing/medical/playerhealth.html

The FIFA website has information about how to get the most out of playing football by eating healthily and avoiding injuries.